The Waiting Season

Raniya Henry

CONTENTS

INTRODUCTION

I would like to thank God for making this book a reality. Hallowed be your name forever and ever. Thank you for seeing me fit to be a vessel to deliver this precious message.

This book was written in the midst of my waiting season. One day, while I was borderline frustrated with waiting, God downloaded the blueprint for everything in my heart. I believe He led me to this writing journey to assist with my waiting season and yours, too! As Christ's followers, we will constantly be placed in waiting seasons that will produce perseverance, faith, and hope.

I pray this book touches and ushers you into God's presence as you expect Him to show up and show out. We serve a mighty God who is forever faithful and never fails.

CHAPTER 1
TIMELY PREPARATION

Waiting on God's promises has to be the most peculiar process known to mankind. You have this promise that you know will come to pass, but it is determined by God's perfect timing. What takes place in the waiting season makes it all profound. It is where your faith is strengthened, your discernment is heightened, and your true love for Christ is revealed. In order to take full advantage of the waiting season, we must spend our time wisely. As we see in Ecclesiastes 3:1;

"To everything there is a season, a time for every purpose under heaven."

While God is not bound by time, being that He is the ancient of days, we are as long as we are in our human bodies. Thankfully, inwardly, we are being renewed every day. One of the biggest misconceptions that believers come into agreement with while in their waiting season is that no work is required. As lovely as that sounds, it is far from the truth. The waiting season does not always equate to physical rest.

Preparation in the waiting season determines what our harvest season will look like. In the natural, many individuals live in places where they must prepare for different seasons. In the winter, they may invest in coats or snow tires, and a few months later, purchase swimsuits and loads of sunscreen for the summer. Others may even have to prepare for hurricane season. As a result, people frantically run to stores to buy countless packs of water, flashlights, toilet paper, and canned food. Therefore, when the weather changes, everything is already arranged to endure and live comfortably.

Let's consider most of the greatest athletes in the world. They will condition their bodies in the off-season to prepare for the actual season. Football players may train for up to seven consecutive months to play at an intense level for five months. Olympic participants may train for an average of four to eight years to perform for a little over two weeks. Additionally, they will commit to a nutritional lifestyle to support their training and performance. In the same way with athletes, we must, too, ensure that we are preparing ourselves while we wait on God's promises. 2 Timothy 4:2 goes on to say;

"Preach the word! Be ready in season and out of season. Convince, rebuke, exhort, with all longsuffering and teaching."

Time and resources can be wasted laboring in vain if you are not on the same accord as God regarding timing. Preparation is a matter of utilizing your time with wisdom, as there will be sacrifices along your journey. For example, God revealed to you through a dream that you would preach to a large crowd within the next few weeks. Instead of going to your friend's birthday dinner, God convicted you to stay home and fast while studying the life of Jesus and what He preached. The preparation season may look like spending an abnormal amount of time in God's presence and studying the word to show yourself approved —

every second counts. Do not take this as an opportunity to be lazy and rub your feet together. Always remember that the harvest is plentiful, but the workers are few (Matthew 9:37).

Proverbs 20:4 reminds us that;

"The lazy man will not plow because of winter; He will beg during harvest and have nothing. "

When we look at the life of Jesus, we can see that He understood times and seasons. While His brothers pressured Him to show Himself to the world and let them see His works, Jesus discerned that the Jewish leaders in Judea were looking for a way to kill him. He then responded to His brothers in John 7:6;

"Then Jesus said to them, 'My time has not yet come, but your time is always ready."

Jesus did not care about the stardom and popularity that His brothers were referring to. He came strictly to do His Father's business. He only went to places He was sent and said what His Father told Him to say. And surely no one would take His life from Him, and certainly not on their own timing.

Then, right before Jesus was about to be handed over to the chief priests and Pharisees, He prayed to God in John 17:1;

> *"... 'Father, the hour has come. Glorify Your Son, that Your Son also may glorify You.'"*

Another reference to timing in the Bible was at the time God told Abraham that He would return at an appointed time the following year and that Sarah would bear a son through which the covenant God made with Abraham would be established. The time was already pre-determined. Genesis 18:14 reads;

> *"Is anything too hard for the Lord? At the appointed time I will return to you, according to the time of life, and Sarah shall have a son."*

God delivered on the promises at the time He promised. Although Sarah was 90 years of age, the world's clock of when women were to bear children or Sarah's unbelief did not restrict God. Despite their old age, God did it for them. Sarah bore a child at the time God had promised Abraham. He is not a delayed or late God, but a punctual and dependable God.

We can see that timing played a vital role in several individuals' journeys throughout the bible. Can you imagine what would have happened had Joseph not advised Pharaoh to prepare during the seven years of great abundance for the famine that was to take place in the following seven years? Or what may have happened had the angels not told Lot to "hurry to leave the city"? Now, keep in mind that even when Lot hesitated, they safely dragged him out of Sodom and Gomorrah. There was an urgency at that moment because God scheduled to destroy the city by raining down burning sulfur on the wicked people.

Lastly, God is the one who changes times and seasons. However, it is important to note that while seasons may change, He still remains the same. You may believe you are not prepared enough to go into your next season, but God may very well be saying you are. Everything that you need is already stored up on the inside of you. The gifts God has given you are already there. It just needs to be birthed.

Maybe God is having you experience growing pains in this season that will eventually force you to grow and expand your territory; either way, you can be confident in the truth that His presence is going with you. He predestined you, which means He determined in advance. He knows when it is time for you to move into your next season. Daniel 2:21 reminds us;

"And He changes the times and the seasons; He removes kings and raises up kings; He gives wisdom to the wise and knowledge to those who have understanding."

In the natural, times and seasons changes may be more evident, like the clock ticking, leaves changing colors, the temperature increasing, and snow melting. However, in the spiritual realm, we must be in constant communication with the Father to be able to discern what season we are currently in and what season is approaching. This will afford you the opportunity to take full advantage of what God is doing in your life.

In my own life, I had to truly understand seasons to fully accept the season I was in and begin to prepare in a timely manner for the next one. While in deep prayer, God revealed that a podcast was something He had for my sister, Radijah, and I in our book of destiny. That podcast would later be called Soft Life Through Christ. Prior to this revelation, we had no experience in the podcasting industry, and while on "paper" we didn't appear qualified, God qualified us. That qualification was not founded upon a degree, certification, or human approval, just a relationship with the Father and a surrendered free will.

Here is something most people do not know, but I will be transparent enough to tell it. After receiving the revelation that we would be hosts of a podcast, we took it upon ourselves to take the easy way out and rent a podcast studio for 2-3 hours to film. Turns out, it was an absolute disaster! We both kept stumbling on our words, our nerves were through the roof, and we did not hit anywhere near the key points we wanted to touch on.

To make matters even worse, when we got home to edit the clips, the audio was ridiculously low and the camera quality was like that of an old-school camera. This situation led us into deep prayer again to seek God and ask Him to reveal the provision He had set up for us. At the end of the day, this was His idea and we are His disciples, so Him being a good father must reveal our next steps. One of the scriptures that reassured me at this time was Luke 22:35;

"And He said to them, 'When I sent you without money, bag, knapsacks, or sandals, did you lack anything?' So they said, 'Nothing.'"

This is where faith enters the chat. We did not give up or slander the promise. Instead, we acknowledged that we operated outside His will and timing, humbled ourselves, and repented. From there, God revealed the correct timing to start preparing and that the podcast would be recorded in our home. That led us to begin searching diligently for the perfect equipment.

Later, I found a YouTube video that detailed everything we would need to get this show on the road. By faith, we started purchasing microphones, a camera, a neon sign, and lightning to film this podcast. Within a few weeks, we had completely built a podcast set. We then asked God to reveal the date we were to publish the podcast, and sure enough, He told us January 20, 2023. A week before that date, we began recording. We started at noon and finished at midnight. We experienced countless technical difficulties that made us grow weary. We went from banking on natural sunlight to later filming in the evening because shadows ruined the set.

No matter how much complaining and border-line crying we did, we still preserved, knowing that God spoke and we were to be obedient. The podcast now sits at over a million collective views on YouTube and over 160,000 downloads on all podcasts applications. Numerous women and men have been delivered and set free from watching, and others got the privilege of hearing about Jesus for the first time. And to this day, we seek God for the exact date to publish each podcast episode. To God be all the glory.

Running the podcast has indeed called for us to fight the good fight of faith. No matter what difficulty we experience, we stand firm knowing that God gave us a promise and His word. God is not a liar. He will do everything He set out to do. It's already written. It's already done!

CHAPTER 2
FAITH

T ruth is, we will not make it in this waiting season without faith in who He is. It takes faith in who God is and His nature to trust and believe in His word. Looking at God's track record, He has never failed. The biblical definition of faith, as described in Hebrews 11:1 is;

"Now faith is the substance of things hoped for, the evidence of things not seen."

Faith can only come from the words that have proceeded from the mouth of God. If you are believing something that did not come from God Himself, then it does not require faith. Faith is an unmerited gift from God. Even if we do not see the manifestation of the things we have faith for, we must maintain hope. If you have to rely on seeing it physically to believe, does that truly depicts faith after all?

Noah, Abraham, Sarah, Isaac, and Jacob had faith until death. They did not get to see the promise manifest into the natural world, but they welcomed it from a distance knowing that they were foreigners and strangers on earth, belonging to a heavenly country. God establishes promises and covenants with you that you have to believe even until death. It will be a generational blessing for your descendants. Just as God repays for the iniquities dating back to the third and fourth generation, how much more will He bless the descendants of those who have been obedient and faithful? For that very reason, do not let your waiting be in vain. Know in your heart that God will upkeep His word even if you never get to see it. Faith calls for us to believe in the things unseen.

A man credited for having "great faith" by Jesus was the centurion. He was a man of authority, with soldiers operating under him. In turn, he understood the authority that Jesus possessed. When the centurion told Jesus that his servant was at home paralyzed, Jesus asked him if He should come and heal Him. In Matthew 8:8;

"The centurion answered and said, "Lord, I am not worthy that You should come under my roof. But only speak a word, and my servant will be healed."

The centurion did not limit the power of Jesus. He had great faith to believe that his servant would be healed if Jesus just spoke the word. He did not need Jesus to come and lay hands on his paralyzed servant. He knew that if he, being a man of authority, could tell his soldiers "go" and "come," how much more could Jesus do? That type of faith could only come from us trusting God. In verse 13, Jesus told him;

"... 'Go your way; and as you have believed, so let it be done for you.' And his servant was healed that same hour. "

We do not have to see the direct manifestation with our human eyes to know that God is moving in the spiritual realm. One of the things God called me out of very early on my faith walk was my business. In June of 2021, I launched a company called Manifest Minks, where I specialized in eyelash extensions and offered comprehensive lash courses. To my surprise, Manifest Minks began to grow at a rapid pace.

Despite the growth of the company, I knew God would not want me in that industry for much longer. After going through deliverance, I went on a fast and asked God to reveal to me the date I was to close my business down. Sure enough, He gave me a vision of the date December 1st, 2022. Coming from being booked and busy every day for a year and a half and making five figures monthly to having little to no source of income was about to be a major financial adjustment. Nonetheless, I remained faithful and trusted God.

It was not until one random day that the Holy Spirit revealed that I should prepare for my next season financially. At this point, it had been six months since I had gone without working, so I must say, I was wondering what God wanted me to budget since I was not working with much.

Knowing and believing that it is impossible to please God without faith and that faith without works is dead, I started to make a budgeting spreadsheet. My background of dropping out of college while studying Business Administration contributed to a portion of the education I had received over the years as I refreshed my knowledge on some accounting principles. I listed my income and expenses along with financial goals, including savings for future businesses and investment opportunities. By faith, I began to prepare for what God would do in my life financially. God had already spoken the word over my life that "eyes have not seen and ears have not heard" what He was about to do for me. So, it wasn't a matter of *if* He would come through for me but a matter of *when*. Even without physical evidence of how this was to happen, I began to brace myself for impact.

I did the work required of me so that when the time came for God to deliver on His promise, I could rest assured that it would be well-stewarded because of the systems put in place amid my waiting season. I understood, then, that obedience required faith. I was able to be obedient because of my faith in God and His unquenchable power.

CHAPTER 3
WILDERNESS

Some may picture the wilderness as an isolated and deserted land that echoes when you speak, while others may imagine it as bushy trees with wild animals. Similar to the natural, the spiritual wilderness is a season of time where you are isolated and being tried by the fire to let God do His finished work in you.

Refining and renewing of the mind takes place during the wilderness period. The refining process prunes you so that you can bear fruit. God is shedding off anything that is not of Him and making us Holy; to be presented blameless before Him. He is replacing our own self-righteousness with His righteousness, our pride with His humility, and our selfishness with His selflessness.

As believers, we are not exempt from this fundamental process. Jesus, Himself, went through the wilderness immediately after being baptized. He was there for 40 days and 40 nights as the enemy tempted him as seen in Mark 1:12-13;

"Immediately the Spirit drove Him into the wilderness. And He was there in the wilderness forty days, tempted by Satan, and was with the wild beasts; and the angels ministered to Him."

You will be tempted by situations and circumstances to ensure your old ways have died off. We must go through the fire! In the natural world, metals undergo a refining process by being placed in scorching temperatures where the dross (impurities) rises to the surface. The dross is then extracted without harming the pure metal. That metal is then used to create many of the products we utilize today. That purification process that takes place for metals is similar to the sanctification process we endure on our journey with Christ. The process uproots anything contrary to what God has spoken and replaces it with the truth, which sets us free.

The blessing of getting tried through the fire is that God is always present fathering us and the angels are there ministering to us. Because God is a father and He loves us, you can expect to be chastened. God will not test you with wickedness but will allow the tests to take place. It is important to note that the test will continuously present itself until you can pass it gracefully. It is not a glamorous process, despite the benefits that come as a result of it. It will reveal flawed characteristics that have been buried as we commit to receiving healing, forgiveness, and deliverance. The Bible reminds us in Hebrews 12:11 that;

"Now no chastening seems to be joyful for the present, but painful; nevertheless, afterward it yields the peaceable fruit of righteousness to those who have been trained by it."

Everyone's wilderness will look different. For some, God may have convicted them to give up all their material possessions because those things fed their ego and made them very prideful, and sub-sequently, became an idol in their lives. For others, it may look like detachment from their close relatives because, in the past, they used them as a crutch for financial support.

Ultimately, the wilderness is predicated on you. Will you be willing to die to yourself and annihilate your own selfish gain? Will you be willing to forsake your family members? Will you be willing to let go of that relationship that God didn't ordain for you? Will you be willing to forfeit the business you worked so tirelessly on?

You have to truly count the cost. What is it going to cost you to be in covenant with Him? There will be worthwhile sacrifices you have to make. Is denying yourself and picking up your cross and following Jesus a priority for you? Remember, you can not serve two masters. You have to choose this day whom you will serve. Both, Jesus and the world, are not an option. Being lukewarm will not cut it anymore. You can not have one foot in and one foot out. It's all or nothing.

It may even appear to be a period of uncertainty in the wilderness but that is why you have to fully depend on God. Trust Him. Trust that He will lead and guide you with perfection and excellence. Not only will there be some uncertainty, but you will be persecuted for your faith and tempted with wickedness. Temptation is not foreign in the wilderness. I would be doing a disservice to you if I made the journey seem like it is always sunshine and rainbows. While I can not guarantee you that it will not storm, I can assure you that a rainbow will come after. What matters most is that you have peace amid the storm, knowing that Jesus can and will tell your life's waves (trials and tribulations) to quiet and be still.

Some individuals will desire to leave the wilderness and go back to Egypt like the Israelites. This defeated mindset clouded their judgment and led them to believe that they were better off being held captive to slavery than experiencing true freedom in Christ. Instead of being dependent on God and trusting Him, they would rather enter an illusion of a safe zone in Egypt. The very same place where they experienced harsh forced labor.

Therefore, we must be intentional about taking upon His divine nature. We will only be prepared for what He promised if we have His divine nature. As believers, we are being conformed into the image of Christ. If we want to refrain from not bearing fruit and being ineffective in our walk with

God, we should subject ourselves to look more and more like Him daily. 2 Peter 1:2-8 displays God's divine nature;

*"Grace and peace be multiplied to you in the knowledge of God and of Jesus our Lord, as His divine power has given to us all things that pertain to life and godliness, through the knowledge of Him who called us by glory and virtue, by which have been given to us exceedingly great and precious promises, that through these you may be partakers of the divine nature, having escaped the corruption that is in the world through lust. But also for this very reason, giving all diligence, add to your **faith virtue**, to virtue **knowledge**, to knowledge **self-control**, to self-control **perseverance**, to perseverance **godliness**, to godliness **brotherly kindness**, and to brotherly kindness **love**. For if these things are yours and abound, you will be neither barren nor unfruitful in the knowledge of our Lord Jesus Christ."*

When you exit the wilderness, you will reflect His glory, and others will surely know you serve a mighty God. You will have developed what some may call an "immunity" to the fire and the flames will not set us ablaze because of our relationship with God. There will be an undeniable transformation that occurs, and you will not want to partake in your old ways anymore. You will begin to see sin how God sees it, and also view yourself and others from the lens of God.

Do not be afraid of the fire but rather embrace it because it exposes the areas we need God's grace to empower us to overcome. When people sin, they tend to go down a rabbit hole, thinking they are doomed forever, therefore, they keep sinning. Simply repent! Commit to change! Be thankful that the fire exposed the areas that need God's grace so that you can, in turn, correct your foundation. It's important to note if the love of Jesus Christ is not your foundation when tried through the fire, the foundation will be exposed once the work is destroyed. 1 Corinthians 3:11-15 tells us;

"For no other foundation can anyone lay than that which is laid, which is Jesus Christ. Now if anyone builds on this foundation with gold, silver, precious stones, wood, hay, straw, each one's work will become clear; for the Day will declare it, because it will be revealed by fire; and the fire will test each one's work,

of what sort it is. If anyone's work which he has built on it endures, he will receive a reward. If anyone's work is burned, he will suffer loss; but he himself will be saved, yet so as through fire."

Can you imagine building a house in a hurricane-prone area and making the executive decision to use straw as your foundation and expect it to still stand when the storm comes? Instead, you will ensure that you use concrete and install hurricane proof windows. How much more of a solid foundation should we desire to have in our relationship with the Lord God almighty?

My refining process was revealed to me as I'm trusting God for what I know will be fulfilled, which is my Kingdom marriage. I have received dreams and visions about this particular gentleman that God ordained for me, stamped with a date that I can expect to be married. While marriage is a beautiful thing and a reflection of our heavenly marriage to come, without the proper foundation, it will not succeed.

Often, when I find myself wanting to skip over some months to get to that promised date, I always have to reflect and tell myself that there is something God is trying to do in me now, but if I get distracted, I will surely miss it. We all can agree that there is work that God does in an individual's singleness that overflows into a marriage. For example, I do not always feel like throwing out the trash or cleaning up messes I did not make. Though valid, my feelings do not determine whether or not these tasks need to be done. Further, they are indispensable in order to uphold a clean and, more importantly, safe house.

Regarding my current household, I only think about the inconvenience it causes me, not considering that maybe my sister may need help, being overwhelmed with motherhood and ministry. Better yet, it will help my future self even if it inconveniences me now. There will be fewer dirty dishes or less stinking trash to throw out later. Though this may all seem superficial, it had been revealed to me that I had some selfish tendencies with a hybrid of laziness. You may wonder, "What does that have to do with marriage?" The truth is, throughout scripture, we can see God calling us to humble ourselves and serve. Male or female. Mother or Father. Husband or wife.

"And whatever you do, do it heartily, as to the Lord and not to men, knowing that from the Lord you will receive the reward of the inheritance; for you serve the Lord Christ" (Colossians 3:23-24).

Now, this is where mindset comes in. If I serve individuals in my household how I serve the Lord, my whole demeanor and heart posture would change. I would do it with pure motives and not to later say, "I did that for you, so you should do this for me." This characteristic is also exercised in Kingdom marriages. If I operate from selfish ambitions, my marriage would be bound for destruction. It's all about dying to self just as we proclaimed we did when we came into covenant with Jesus. Jesus is the standard. The way He loved, served, and sacrificed should be the standard to what I hold myself up to. The Bible tells us in 1 John 4:17 that,

"Love has been perfected among us in this: that we may have boldness in the day of judgment; because as He is, so are we in this world."

Having come to that realization, I began to serve those in my home as if Jesus was living there. God began to purge the selfishness I developed over the years and replaced it with selflessness. Now, there are things I do for others that they do not even see, and while it may not produce recognition, then great is my reward in Heaven.

CHAPTER 4

IDENTITY

One of the most beautiful things that transpire in the waiting season is that God will set you apart and consecrate you to prepare you for your assignment. There are things that He wants to give birth to that require separation. If we do not endure this process, we will abort the spiritual gifts and assignments that God has placed on the inside of us.

John the Baptist was a great illustration of God separating someone to give birth to something great. Before birth, John was special and anointed, leaping in his mother, Elizabeth's womb, right before she was filled with the Holy Spirit. Elizabeth was in seclusion for five months, precisely after she became pregnant. John eventually grew up and prepared the way for our Lord and Savior, Jesus Christ. With such an important calling, God needed to consecrate him in the wilderness for years and away from people that could have plotted to kill or rob him of his destiny because, since birth, people in Judea knew that the Lord's hand was on John.

Sometimes, we will not be able to go to certain places or attend certain functions because God has set us apart in this season to do His will. Even if these functions promote God, we must always prioritize our relationship with Him over everything and everyone. People will look at you as though you have lost your mind because it is unfamiliar to them. You will quickly realize that although we live *in* this world, we are not *of* this world. We are foreigners and strangers here because our permanent residence is in the Kingdom of Heaven. Therefore, we must set our minds on things above, not on earthly things (Colossians 3:2).

Depending on your circumstances, this can include separating yourself from family and friends for the time being. Many times, those closest to you can hinder you along your journey because they can not see past who you used to be. The same way people from Jesus' hometown questioned where He got His power from because He was the carpenter's son and began to point out who His earthly family members were. This lack of honor and faith led to Him not being able to perform as many miracles there. People operating from their natural minds are not going to be able to understand why you think and act the way you do.

While it may temporarily sting, we ought to look at the bigger picture. God knows the beginning from the end; there is always a valid reason attached to His why. In this time, God wants to get you alone and away from distractions. We often may feel like we are missing out on things or falling behind when we are consecrating, but remember, God can make what would typically take ten years to do, be completed in ten days.

When I received salvation in October of 2022, I immediately went into consecration. What I witnessed during those three days of deliverance transformed my life. I deleted all forms of my social media and only came out of the house if it was for work, bible study, or assisting with deliverances. I informed my friends that I could not hang out with them for some time or have extra guests at my lash studio. In those days, I felt separated from the world. When I would go out places, I would feel alienated and different. My spiritual eyes and ears were opened, and I could not view the natural things the same way as before. I realized that many of the things I attached myself to were demonic; from the music I listened to down to the clothing I wore.

As I was consecrating, God began to work on my identity. I got the privilege of spending time with Him and got to know my true identity in Christ. I learned that I am an ambassador of Christ, fearfully and wonderfully made, a minister of reconciliation, a saint, and I am born again of the incorruptible seed of the word of God. I had to actively train my mind as though I was training for the military. This called for me to renew my mind daily to match with everything God said about me. The word of God is the only way to do such. The Word is indeed sharp, active, and still applicable to our lives today. Whenever I think or hear anything contrary to what God called me to be, I counter-claim it immediately with the truth through God's Holy Word.

Along with my identity, I discovered that I enjoy writing, reading new novels, building 300-piece puzzles, editing videos, and traveling worldwide. These same things that I discovered are what the enemy tried to rob me of when I was in the world system. But thankfully, God snatched it back and is using it for the Kingdom of Light now. There are things that God has revealed to me and continues to reveal to me in my consecration period that I treasure. Not only was God providing me with fresh revelation during this time, but He was also showing me that He was preparing me for what was to come. I would see visions of a kitchen or utensils as if I was preparing to eat a meal.

Now, this is huge for me because I used to fear being alone; I actually hated being alone. I feared being trapped in my own self-deprecated thoughts. Those thoughts were flooded with lies from the enemy, causing me to believe I was not enough and needed someone outside of Jesus. Even as I worked, I would always have a podcast playing in the background or a family member on the phone, if I was not conversing with my client. I rarely had quiet time to sit in my thoughts and hear God's voice. Even on the drive home, I would blast my music to escape from the feeling of loneliness. I let loneliness and low self-worth keep me from experiencing the Father's steadfast love. No matter how successful my company got or how much my family reassured me that they loved me, I still felt a void. I even enrolled in therapy for a few months, but nothing seemed to do. A piece of the puzzle was missing.

I could remember writing journal entries during the time when I felt like my sin had separated me from God. I had this hope that I would eventually surrender everything I was holding tightly to God but my mind was not renewed and I did not believe that God's grace could turn me from my sinful ways.

December 30, 2019

This love stuff is really a drug, or maybe I'm crazy. It makes me scared. My fear is that I'll love so hard and lose myself for good. I already started losing myself little by little. Love makes me feel happy and sad on the same day. And soul ties make it worse. I feel EVERYTHING. I got to find a way to love but not let it consume me. I know the answer is through God, but it's something I'm avoiding. I keep yelling at Him, praying that He will hear me, but I need to learn to listen and be obedient. I keep thinking stuff is "ok" because I'm young, but it will never be ok and acceptable. Everybody I talk to tells me it's ok and I'm just overthinking, but I know the truth. I feel so weak but strong. Strong because I'm getting through this but weak because I put myself through this. I'm excited for the new year, but if I take the realistic approach, I'm going in with the same weight as 2019. I don't know how to let it down. I know I'll read back on this one day and wish I had told myself to calm down and that everything would work itself out. I'll want to tell this little girl that better is coming. Your tears are being used to water seeds. You are loved by God. Everything you need, you have. You are healed by the healer. Your broken heart is repaired, baby girl. Just breathe.

Friday, April 10, 2020

I think I have it figured out. Today while watching a video, "How to fall in love again," she said, "You're gonna have to fall in love with the person you're going to ultimately spend the rest of your life with—yourself." That hit it for me. I truly believe that a part of my current relationship failing is because I don't love myself enough to do what is best for me. To leave when it is no longer working, to stand up for what I believe in, and don't fear being alone with myself. Don't get me wrong. I love me. I'm not as insecure as he makes me out to be. I know I'm strong, courageous, smart, and beautiful, but I really fear being alone because of the consequences of not caring for myself [mentally, spiritually, and physically]. I want to love and nurture me.

I try to do that for others, but they won't receive it until later, and hopefully, it's not too late. I do have flaws within this relationship, but I'm working on it because I'm willing to take the steps necessary to improve the relationship; that way, if it doesn't work out, at least I know I did my part. Well, I plan to work on myself a little more. I will use all the energy and time I invested into this relationship for myself. I think it's time to open up my lash shop and flourish. It's also time to rekindle my relationship with God because all my plans will fail if I don't have his approval. Lord, there's so much I want to change, but I'm going to take it one step at a time and day by day.

Lately, the world has been stuck in quarantine because of the pandemic. I've been working, so I've been able to stay sane, but I know things have to get worse before they get better, unfortunately. I'm cautious, but I'm not worried because fear will just corrupt my mind and weaken my immune system. Sometimes I wonder why sickness exists. No disrespect to God, but He has the power to make it all go away and never kill people. I don't know, but I really would like to know. This diary has helped me tremendously. Sometimes I flip through the pages and remember how hurt I was and even how happy I used to be, like when I got my first job or finally bought my first car. I want to get back to that level of joy, but as you age, you experience and witness more, so it's hard to act like an innocent child. I miss my old self, but I would never get her back, so I must embrace the new me and make her into a dope butterfly.

***

Now that I have truly accepted Christ into my heart, there is not a day that goes by that I feel lonely. Even when the enemy attempts to whisper lies in my head, I remind myself of the truth in God's word. How can I believe I'm lonely when I have 24/7 access to the Lord of all Lords and the King of all Kings? The veil has been torn! There's absolutely nothing between the bride (us) and the bridegroom (Jesus) that prevents us from being in relationship. That does not sound lonely to me! It sounds like I have a father and friend for eternity! You can not enter the Lord's presence defeated and lacking a grasp of your identity. You have to know who you are and whose you are!

To think that my fear of being lonely in the past would have kept me from this moment makes me view things differently. Now, I can proudly say, I thoroughly enjoy consecration. Almost too much. Venturing into a quiet place where it's just me and God is so intimate. While on the outside looking in, it may appear lonesome; I constantly feel like God is wrapping His arms around me and embracing me in those moments. There are no words to describe the feeling accurately; you would have to experience it.

CHAPTER 5
COUNTERFEITS

"Catch us the foxes, the little foxes that spoil the vines,
for our vines have tender grapes"
(Song of Solomon 2:15).

Previously, I would think of compromise as this far-fetched ordeal, like a Christian converting to an atheist. But on the contrary, it is the small things known as the "little foxes" in scripture that people often brush under the rug. We ought to be mindful of how compromise enters because we can find ourselves giving in to a counterfeit version of the promise God has us waiting for. The crafty thing about counterfeits is that it is presented disguised as the real thing on the outside, but deep down, it is all lies and deceit.

Think about how often people have been bam-boozled by people selling fake luxury items. Those desiring a luxury handbag may fall for the seller's low prices and relatively close matching to the designer items without ever knowing that the bag is not authentic. Just as there are dupe versions of designer bags, there is a false Holy Spirit, false prophets, false teachings, false apostles, false signs and wonders, false messiahs, and false doctrines. Satan is a copycat. He desires to copy everything that God has done. The enemy even knows scrip-ture but twists it to get people to stumble in their ignorance and think that evil is good and good is evil. He desires to choke the Word of God out of you. His assignment is to steal, kill, and destroy.

"And no wonder! For Satan himself transforms himself into an angel of light. Therefore it is no great thing if his ministers also transform themselves into ministers of righteousness, whose end will be according to their works" (2 Corinthians 11:14-15).

Although counterfeits will come packaged sim-ilarly to what God promised you, by using your discernment and testing the spirit by the word of God, you will know if it is not what God has for you.

My counterfeit encounter was with a gentleman I considered a friend, despite his attempts to date me for several years. One day, he confessed to me that he believed God had shown him that I was his wife. I kindly told him that this revelation contradicted the revelations I received from God and that I knew I was not his wife. Based on the similar physical features, I could have easily been confused and questioned God, asking, "Well, which one is truly my husband?" but I knew that God is not the author of confusion.

Therefore, what took place was simply a distraction. The enemy despises Kingdom marriages, and he will fabricate crafty schemes to detour you from what God has for you. When a counterfeit version of the promise is revealed, you must rejoice, knowing that what God truly promised is coming near. It simply entails that the real version is on its way!

I must admit, I was not always so sharp about not compromising in the past. At the age of 16, I attended a purity ball where I established a covenant with God to wait until marriage to have sex. This covenant was not only about sex but living a life of purity. As time passed, I started to compromise with the type of music I listened to, and I felt so separated from God because I never truly grasped the difference between condemnation versus conviction. Music led to drinking, drinking led to cursing, cursing led to dressing provocatively, and dressing provocatively led to meeting men in darkness, which led to sex outside of marriage. Before you know it, I was in complete darkness. I felt separated from God in those times because my sin seemed so far-fetched and unforgivable.

The relationship I traded God for was outright toxic and below what I was deserving of. However, I somehow felt I deserved that treatment because I had breached my covenant with God. Knowing what I know now, I would have understood that repentance was vital in those moments. I had to change my thought pattern about those sins. Thankfully, now, I know nothing can separate me from the love of God through Jesus Christ. Those incidents should have ushered me even more into God's presence because His grace is powerful and sufficient to turn me away from those sins. That is why I have now entirely closed doors in my life that would lead to compromise because I never want to even think I'm separated from God like that ever again.

Renewing my celibacy vow to God has brought forth so much peace. Walking in purity has allowed me to keep my mind on the matters of the Kingdom and not be distracted by the desires of my flesh. It feels amazing to honor God with my body considering that it is a temple housing the Holy Spirit. Sexual sins such as fornication and lust come with consequences such as spiritual death, soul ties, sick- nesses, and children out of wedlock to name a few. Waiting until marriage will be worth the wait. Always remember that it is better to wait for what God has for you than to rush into what He does not have for you. Rushing is anti-kingdom!

CHAPTER 6
WAIT IN EXPECTATION

Don't affirm doubts of the promise coming to pass. If you believe God spoke it, then stand on that in faith. God's word tells us to consider it "pure joy" when our faith is tested because that produces perseverance. We need perseverance on this walk with God, and after having stood the test, you will receive the crown of life that He promised to those who love Him. Learning to endure through the good and the bad matures and completes us in our faith. The one who does doubt should not expect to receive anything from the Lord, and He refers to those people as "double-minded and unstable in all his ways" (James 1:8).

The most pivotal waiting season we are in is anticipating Christ's return. His word has already gone out, and we know it will come to pass. Jesus Christ is returning! He is coming for His bride! 2 Peter 3:11-13 states that we can look forward to a new heaven and new earth where righteousness dwells.

"Therefore, since all these things will be dissolved, what manner of persons ought you to be in holy conduct and godliness, looking for and hastening the coming of the day of God, because of which the heavens will be dissolved, being on fire, and the elements will melt with fervent heat? Nevertheless we, according to His promise, look for new heavens and a new earth in which righteousness dwells."

The spirit of the antichrist attempts to downplay the authenticity of this return which God addresses in verse 4; "... *Where is the promise of His coming? For since the fathers fell asleep, all things continue as they were from the beginning of creation."*

Many people conclude that it will no longer take place, focusing on the number of years since it was first prophesied. But verse 8 and 9 lets us know that we can stay encouraged and wait in expectation for that day will undoubtedly come.

"But, beloved, do not forget this one thing, that with the Lord one day is as a thousand years, and a thousand years as one day. The Lord is not slack concerning His promise, as some count slackness, but is longsuffering toward us, not willing that any should perish but that all should come to repentance."

How much of a loving Father do we serve that He is waiting on those lost sheep to come to repentance rather than seeing them perish into eternal suffering? We should thank Him for that. Christ, the bridegroom, wants to present us, the bride, holy, blameless, and blemish-free to the Father.

What if I challenge you to consider that, just maybe, God is waiting on us? Let's take, for example, the Israelites who stayed in the wilderness for 40 years due to their complaints and unbelief that ultimately led to false god worship. God desired to deliver them from the Egyptians and place them in the Promised Land flowing with milk and honey. Unfortunately, complaining and unbelief create open portals for the enemy to deceive. Complaining removes your heart from a postured position to receive the truth and submit to the Lord. They become so stuck on their emotions and circumstances that they lost sight of who He is. In Hosea 4:16, we see the stubbornness of the Israelites.

"For Israel is stubborn
Like a stubborn calf;
Now the Lord will let them forage
Like a lamb in open country."

Truth is, if we are not walking by the spirit, many individuals can easily take on the Israelites' mindset while God is trying to do new things in our lives. We have been promised a new heaven and new earth, which will come very soon. But God, being the loving, gracious Father that He is, is affording everyone the opportunity of a lifetime to come to repentance. He has not forgotten what He promised us. Further, His time is not measured as our sense of time is. A thousand years to us is just a day to Him. Therefore, do not think that God is delayed in keeping His promise.

Even in the days of Noah, with whom God established His covenant, God patiently waited as Noah built the ark. God gave Noah specific instructions on how to fashion the ark and who and what was to be occupying it. God was not slow in keeping His promise. Instead, 1 Peter 3:20 shows us that God waited on Noah to complete the assignment;

"who formerly were disobedient, when once the Divine longsuffering waited in the days of Noah, while the ark was being prepared, in which a few, that is, eight souls, were saved through water."

It is God's will to be gracious to us. He wants to give us the promises He has spoken of. If He did not, He would not make them. It is God's good pleasure to give His sheep the Kingdom. He is the ultimate shepherd, tending and providing for the needs of His sheep.

"Therefore the Lord will wait, that He may be gracious to you; And therefore He will be exalted, that He may have mercy on you. For the Lord is a God of justice; Blessed are all those who wait for Him" (Isaiah 30:18).

***

Intercession is vital if there seems to be a hindrance or delay as you are waiting for God's word to come to pass. First, we must remember that we have an advocate with the Father, Jesus, who is at the right hand of God and is also interceding for us. Intercession is the process of intervening or petitioning on behalf of another. This can intel placing God in remembrance of the promise He gave you and quote His word back to Him. Isaiah 43:26 reads,

"Put Me in Remembrance;
Let us contend together;
State your case, that you may be acquitted."

Consider here in Exodus 32:13-14 when Moses reminded God of what He had spoken:

"Remember Abraham, Isaac, and Israel, Your
servants, to whom You swore by Your own self, and said
to them, 'I will multiply your descendants as the stars
of heaven; and all this land that I have spoken of I give
to your descendants, and they shall inherit it forever.'

So the LORD relented from the harm which He said He would do to His people."

Moses stood in the gap for the Israelites when God was going to send His wrath and destroy them for making a gold idol to sacrifice and worship after they were brought out of captivity in Egypt. Moses, having reminded God of the promise He swore to Abraham, Isaac, and Israel, was able to save the Israelites from destruction and now keep God's agenda flowing. His intercession fashioned God to backpedal and reconsider destroying the Israelites. Isaiah 62:7 demonstrates how we ought to *"give the Lord no rest"* until He establishes what He said He was to establish. His word shall come to pass and not return to Him void. We must war with the prophecies we have received from God. That is how we will fight the battle well. Remember what God spoke to you and use it to fuel your determination to bring heaven on Earth.

While writing this book that you are reading, I experienced what most people call "writer's block" for a solid week. Now if you know anything about the timeline God gave me for when this book was to be executed, you would know I did not have a week, a day, an hour, a minute, or a second to spare.

After realizing that my "writer's block" was not coming from the Lord, I entered my prayer closet and began to war with the prophecy of this task God had given me. I started by reminding God that He wrote this Kingdom assignment He had given me in my destiny book. In addition, I reminded Him about all the prophecies and dreams I had received about it.

Then, I proceeded to cast down any hindrances or delays that were trying to come up against the book from being written. Finally, by the power invested in me through Jesus Christ, I canceled the enemy's assignment and thanked God in advance for what He was about to do through the book. The daily bread I received from God the following morning was "rest assured," and sure enough, by the next day, I was back on my way, writing like nothing ever happened.

I could have easily stayed in agreement with writer's block and delayed the book by several more days. But God is so much of a loving father that He revealed to me what was taking place spiritually so that I could ascend and pray against the principalities and rulers of darkness' assignment. That is how true kingdom citizens operate. You do not mope in sadness and leave the Lord's kingdom assignments unaccomplished. No. We hold on to the word spoken to us and use the authority and power Christ left to us to overcome the schemes of wickedness.

"Let us, therefore, come boldly to the throne of grace, that we may obtain mercy and find grace to help in time of need" (Hebrews 4:16).

CHAPTER 7

Don't pervert the promise

While in the waiting season, we must place insurance on the truth that we love God for nothing. Before Satan was granted access to torment God's faithful servant, Job, he asked the Lord, "Does Job fear God for nothing?" One of the constant reminders that I tell myself is, "Even if what I'm waiting or praying for never happens, He's still good." This heart posture has kept me from unhealthily obsessing over the promises but focusing on who is the one who distributes the promise. Remembering James 1:17 reads;

"Every good gift and every perfect gift is from above, and comes down from the Father of lights, with whom there is no variation or shadow of turning."

Keeping your eyes fixated on Jesus eliminates distractions, self-righteousness, and ill motives. Be so consumed by God's goodness that you *almost* do not even recognize that you have entered the Promised Land. We will often find that what seems like God did not deliver on a promise reveals the intention behind what someone was seeking the promise for.

For instance, the story of Shadrach, Meshach, and Abednego, who embraced the fire they were placed in. King Nebuchadnezzar was furious that they would not bow down and serve his false gods or worship an image of gold he set up. Therefore, he demanded that they be tied up and thrown into a blazing furnace and ordered to have the temperature heated seven times hotter than usual. How they responded in Daniel 3:17-18 to the persecution was remarkable:

"If that is the case, our God whom we serve is able to deliver us from the burning fiery furnace, and He will deliver us from your hand, O king. But if not, let it be known to you, O king, that we do not serve your gods,

nor will we worship the gold image which you have set up."

While facing persecution, they remained firm on their foundation of who God is. Even if the persecution led to death, they would not compromise. We have to get to a place on our walk where we are so sold about Jesus that even *if* He does not deliver on His promise, we stand firm on our faith in Him. We can not allow what takes place in the natural to waver what we believe in our hearts about Him.

As a matter of fact, the promise is not even for you. Everything God gives us is for His name's sake! We were designed and created to be glory carriers for His Kingdom. So, our desire should be that when God blesses us with anything, whether it is the spiritual gift of healing, a new car, a new apartment, or a miracle child, the end goal should be that the gift will be used to bring Him back the glory. Many individuals are operating as wolves in sheep's clothing that utilize what God has given them to bring them glory and fund their own hidden agenda. However, the heart posture behind it always gets revealed.

Can you imagine how our heavenly Father feels

when we credit ourselves for things He has done for us? Can you imagine how it pained Him when the Israelites decided to build false idols to worship after He delivered them out of Egypt, provided them with manna daily, a pillar of cloud in the day, and a pillar of fire at night?

In that same way, the beautiful child that God blessed you with after years of barrenness was to multiply His image and likeness. Perhaps your experience would be utilized as a testimony of God's faithfulness to other married couples being attacked by demonic spirits trying to hinder them from childbearing. The Bible reminds us in 1 Peter 4:10;

"As each one has received a gift, minister it to one another, as good stewards of the manifold grace of God."

Pride will cause us to believe our work and efforts generated this harvest season. Our prayer should be that our humility multiplies and intensifies as God continues to elevate us. In every season, we will have a need for God. There will never be a season God places us in where His presence will not be required. In fact, the more we elevate, the more of God we need. We will begin to seek God for fresh revelation and answers. He desires for us to acknowledge Him in all our ways.

"God, how do I steward this ministry? God, what do I do with the people you have assigned to me in this season? Should I sign this deal with this specific real estate investor to generate Kingdom wealth? What did this dream mean last night when I was running with a sword in my hand?" That is the communication God desires—one where our hearts are continuously postured after His.

Let's take, for example, Solomon. God blessed Solomon with supernatural wisdom and greater riches than any other king. God even told him in 1 Kings 9:5, He would establish Solomon's royal throne over Israel forever, as He promised David, his Father. Later, Solomon began to operate outside of God's will. He intermarried with women who worshipped other gods. He began to burn incense and offered sacrifices to their gods. 1 Kings 11:9 tells us;

"The Lord became angry with Solomon because his heart had turned away from the LORD, the God of Israel, who had appeared to him twice."

Our prayers should be that whatever we are waiting on God for should usher us into His presence more than before. We should not want to go anywhere or receive anything if it will turn our hearts away from God, or take us out of His presence. No position, no amount of money, or no person is worth compromising the Lord's presence.

CHAPTER 8
STEWARDSHIP

The promise that God you are trusting God for is going to require proper stewardship. So often, we limit stewardship to finances; however, with the partnership of wisdom from the Holy Spirit, you will be able to steward the word God gave you correctly once it comes to fruition.

I love the parable in Matthew 25:14, about the master and the bags of gold. The master entrusted his servants with his wealth. Each servant was trusted with a certain amount of gold according to their ability. The servant that received five bags of gold doubled it and gained five more, and the one that received two bags of gold doubled it and brought back two more. They both received a *"well done"* from the master and were told they would be put in charge of many things because they were faithful with a few things and were invited to share in their master's joy. Meanwhile, the servant who received one bag of gold hid it in the ground and did nothing with it. Guess what? The one bag of gold was taken from him by the master and given to the one with ten bags. Now, even what he does not possess will be taken from him.

Just like the servants in this parable, we must provide an account of what we did with what God has given us, whether that be souls for the Kingdom or gifts that God has distributed to us. In John 17:12, we can see that Jesus properly stewarded and shepherded the souls God assigned to Him.

"While I was with them in the world, I kept them in Your name. Those whom You gave Me I have kept; and none of them is lost except the son of perdition, that the Scripture might be fulfilled."

What will you do with what God has given you? Will you use it to advance His Kingdom? While God loves everyone the same, there are some that

He trusts with His Kingdom assignments more than others. Therefore, we should all desire to be trusted by our Heavenly Father to carry out His will!

One night, my sister and I were sitting in our apartment, and we started to get uncomfortable in the season we were in. We had been discussing moving out into our own separate apartments so that I could have the opportunity to experience living on my own before I got married. So, I began to schedule numerous apartment tours and started obsessively pinning creative apartment inspiration on Pinterest.

A few days later, the Holy Spirit gave me this instant revelation that while I became hyper focused on the next season, God wanted me to appreciate what I had now. After telling my sister what God convicted me about, we instantly repented. From that point forward, we decided we would alter the words that proceeded out of our mouths in reference to the apartment we were currently staying at. We even took the initiative to go to the store and purchase cute flowers and swap the couch for one I had just sitting in my mother's garage. We added some faux plants on the balcony, and before you knew it, we refreshed our current living space. Seeing what a simple mindset shift can do in your life is quite impressive.

When I repented for complaining about the apartment, I changed my perspective of how I would view it. The decorations were just a bonus for my liking, but it made a huge difference. This pivotal moment reminded me of when Jesus fed the multitude of people. His disciples came to Him with a suggestion to send the crowd away so they could purchase food. Jesus simply asked the disciples how many loaves of bread they had right then. He took the loaves, gave thanks, broke them, and began to feed the large crowd. He did not murmur or complain. In fact, He used what they possessed right there at that moment and multiplied it. With five loaves of bread and two fish, they were able to feed five thousand plus people with some still left over.

Mind renewal was necessary for this situation because I did not want to get consumed by my feelings about my current position, which would cloud what I heard from the Lord. My emotions would have led me to think that God wanted me to move out that month, but I wanted to ensure that I stayed in order with His plans and purpose for my life.

"And do not be conformed to this world, but be transformed by the renewing of your mind, that you may prove what is that good and acceptable and perfect will of God" (Romans 12:2).

Now that we have done that, we are not as aggressive in our approach to moving. Occasionally, we would reference it for preparation purposes, but at that moment, we learned a critical Kingdom lesson about stewardship. We appreciated what we had, which communicated to God that we were grateful for what He had provided us and that whenever He decided to move us, we would be ready. But for now, we chose to bask in His goodness.

I chose that day that I would not wait for Him to put me in a position or place to thank and appreciate Him for what I have. No. I decided to do it right at that moment. So, I challenge you today as you are seeking and thanking God for spiritual gifts, new apartments, new friendships, or new career opportunities to take an audit on your life. Have you stewarded what He has already given to you well? If your answer is yes, great. May God excel you into your next season. If your answer is no, ask the Holy Spirit to reveal to you how you could better steward what He has given you. Once He does, make the necessary changes.

CHAPTER 9
SELAH

S elah is a Hebrew word found over 74 times in the bible specifically in the books of Psalm and Habakkuk. While often used as a music notation to pause, it should simultaneously compel us to take a moment to pause and reflect on God's goodness. Ponder on His divine nature. Let it settle in. Rest in the truth that He is sovereign, just, righteous, faithful, forgiving, loving, holy, and a promise keeper. He has never failed. Not once. He never will fail. He is steadfast.

"For My yoke is easy, and My burden is light"
(Matthew 11:30).

Give Him the praise for what He has already done and praise Him in advance for what He will do. The same God that did it for Abraham, Isaac, and Jacob is the same yesterday, today, and forever. He does not change. Rest assured that He keeps His covenant of love to those who love Him and keep His commandments.

Enter the Lord's rest by faith in Jesus Christ. Release the burden of trying to control this season of your life. Allow God to shepherd you. Listen to His voice to receive direction on what He desires for you to do next. Before He formed you, He knew you. He knew what you would be doing now and He knows what you will be doing next. It was already written. The work He did on the cross is already complete! It is finished! His plan far exceeds the one we have in our minds. He is a master planner, strategic in all His ways. Rest today knowing that God is working everything out for the good of those who love Him.

All God's promises are "Yes" & "Amen" in Christ (2 Corinthians 1:20). Christ is the yes. In other words, He is the guarantee, the warranty, the confirmation, and the assurance. The Hebrew meaning for amen is certainty. Amen is the response to come into agreement with the word spoken and communicate that we are certain of it coming to pass. It binds it up in Heaven and loses it on Earth. It displays that we trust God and that His promises will indeed come into fruition.

I encourage you today to be intentional and write down a list of characteristics of God on one half of a page and on the other side, write a list of things He already has done for you that you are grateful for. May this exercise place you in remembrance and gratitude toward the Heavenly Father.

The Waiting Season

Stay encouraged and stay blessed as you wait on God's promises, Kingdom Family.

ABOUT THE AUTHOR

Raniya Henry is a vibrant author who joyfully embraces her calling as a conduit of divine inspiration. She firmly believes that she is God-ordained to write books for the Kingdom of God, a mission she approaches with passion and zeal. Raniya's dynamic personality shines through as she embraces a fun-loving and adventurous spirit. From unraveling puzzles to exploring new destinations, she finds joy in the intricacies of life. As a co-host of the popular podcast, "Soft Life Through Christ," Raniya showcases the true essence of living a fulfilling and purpose-driven existence. Her journey as a believer, writer, and mentor is fueled by an unwavering determination and a profound desire to transform lives.

Stay Connected

Instagram
www.Instagram.com/Raniyamonae
Youtube
www.Youtube.com/SoftLifeThroughChrist

Made in the USA
Columbia, SC
02 July 2024

37910141R00046